21st
Century
Skills Library

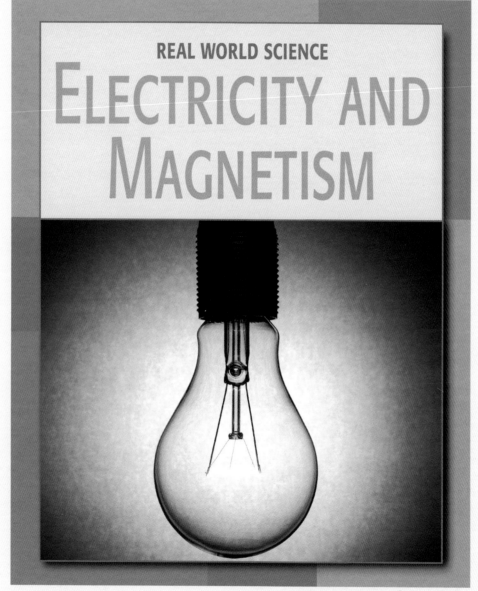

REAL WORLD SCIENCE

ELECTRICITY AND MAGNETISM

Dana Meachen Rau

Cherry Lake Publishing
Ann Arbor, Michigan

CHERRY
LAKE
Publishing

Published in the United States of America by Cherry Lake Publishing
Ann Arbor, Michigan
www.cherrylakepublishing.com

Content Adviser: Laura Graceffa, middle school science teacher; BA degree in science, Vassar College; MA degrees in science and education, Brown University

Photo Credits: Cover and page 1, © Shutterstock; page 4, © BobbyDeal/RealDealPhoto/ Shutterstock; page 6, © Shutterstock; page 8, Katykin/Photo Researchers, Inc.; page 9, © Maldix/Shutterstock; page 11, GIPhotoStock/Photo Researchers, Inc.; page 13, © Andrjuss/Shuttertock; page 14, © Peter Guess/Shutterstock; page 16, Doug Martin/ Photo Researchers, Inc.; page 18, © Feng Yu/Shutterstock; page 19, Joel Arem/Photo Researchers, Inc.; page 21, Charles D. Winters/Photo Researchers, Inc.; page 23, Cordelia Molloy/Photo Researchers, Inc.; page 24, Martin Bond/Photo Researchers, Inc.; page 25, Doug Martin/Photo Researchers, Inc.; page 27, © Oralleff/Shutterstock

Library of Congress Cataloging-in-Publication Data

Rau, Dana Meachen, 1971-
Electricity and magnetism / Dana Meachen Rau.
    p. cm.— (Real world science)
Includes bibliographical references and index.
ISBN-13: 978-1-60279-459-7
ISBN-10: 1-60279-459-6
1. Electricity—Juvenile literature. 2. Magnetism—Juvenile literature.
I. Title. II. Series.

QC527.2.R376 2009
537—dc22   2008045711

*Cherry Lake Publishing would like to acknowledge the work of
The Partnership for 21st Century Skills.
Please visit www.21stcenturyskills.org for more information.*

TABLE OF CONTENTS

CHAPTER ONE

ALL CHARGED UP! INSIDE AN ATOM

Static electricity can make your hair stand on end.

Wake up and start the day! Turn on a light. Toast a bagel. Get juice from

the fridge. You need electricity to do all of these things. Now get dressed. Pull

a sweater over your head. Does your hair stand on end? That is electricity, too!

There are two types of electricity. The kind that makes your hair stand up

is **static electricity**. The kind that flows from a wall outlet is **electric current**.

For both types, something flows from one place to another to create power. So what makes electricity?

Electricity starts with atoms. Atoms make up everything in the world. All things you can see and touch are made of atoms. Even things you can't see, such as air, are made of atoms. They are the basic building blocks of matter. But an atom is made up of even smaller parts. It has a center called a nucleus. This nucleus holds **protons**. **Electrons** circle around the center at very fast speeds. Think of a merry-go-round. The center stays in one place. That's like the center of an atom that holds the protons. All of the horses on the merry-go-round circle around the

Atoms are so small that you can't even see them with a regular microscope. Scientists use special tools to study them. Even though atoms are so small, they are very powerful. An atom bomb is one of the most destructive weapons in history. The explosion of an atom bomb is caused by splitting the center of atoms. These atoms can release enough energy to destroy a whole city. The United States dropped atomic bombs on two cities in Japan in 1945. This action was taken to end World War II. The bombing of Hiroshima and Nagasaki nearly destroyed both cities.

Two electrical charges show that electric current travels in paths.

center. They are like the electrons. But the electrons in an atom don't just take one path around the center. And some electrons are closer to the nucleus than others. The electrons are like a cloud around the center of the atom.

Protons and electrons each hold a little electric power. This power is called a **charge**. Protons have a positive charge. Electrons have a negative charge. An atom has a balanced charge when it has the same amount of protons and electrons.

But some electrons are not as tightly bound to their center as merry-go-round horses. Some electrons can break free from their atoms.

Electricity is created when freed electrons move. Electrons can move from one atom to another. They can also flow from one object to another. An atom is no longer balanced if it loses or gains electrons. It is positively charged if it has more protons than electrons. It is negatively charged if it has more electrons than protons.

Mg   Cu

REAL WORLD SCIENCE CHALLENGE

Li

Be

Turn on your television. It's not time to watch a show. It's time to do an experiment. Take a piece of paper and place it on the screen. The paper should stick to the screen. Why does it stick?

(Turn to page 29 for the answer)

Rb   Na   Fe

Electrons circle around the center of an atom.

Atoms may be small, but they hold a lot of power. We use the electrical

power of atoms every day.

CHAPTER TWO

READY, SET, FLOW! ELECTRONS ON THE MOVE

A bolt of lightning is another kind of static electricity.

Have you ever seen a lightning storm? A bolt of lightning is a zap of static

electricity. Lightning is electricity moving from one place to another in the

sky or from the sky to the ground. Static electricity is created on a smaller

scale when you rub two objects together. The rubbing makes electrons move.

Have you ever walked across a carpet on a dry day? If you touch

a doorknob, you might feel a shock. You may even see a tiny zap of "lightning" between your finger and the doorknob. Electrons travel from

the carpet to you as you walk on it. Then electrons travel from you to the

doorknob when you touch it.

REAL WORLD SCIENCE CHALLENGE

Amaze your friends with this science trick. Take a plastic knife and rub it back and forth on a wool sweater or hat. Run the sink faucet with a very small but steady stream. Wave your plastic "wand" close to the stream of water. The water will bend toward your wand! Why is the water attracted to the wand?

(Turn to page 29 for the answer)

Different charges make objects act in certain ways. Objects that have

the same charge (either positive or negative) will push away from each

other. Objects that have opposite charges (one positive and one negative)

will pull closer to each other. Comb your hair on a dry day. This makes

electrons flow from your hair to the comb. Now the comb is negatively charged. Hold the comb close to small pieces of tissue paper. The tissue paper will move toward the comb. Why does this happen? The positive charges in the paper pull closer to the negative charges in the comb.

Negatively charged electrons cause bits of tissue paper to stick to a comb.

Static electricity is caused by moving electrons. So is electric current. But the electrons move in different ways in each. Imagine you are going out for recess with your class. Your teacher opens the door, and everyone runs out. They scatter to all different places on the playground. That is like how electrons move in static electricity. In electric current, electrons are more organized. Imagine you are walking down the hall with your class.

Your teacher asks you to walk in single file. You all move forward along the same path. That is like the flow of electrons in an electric current. Electric current is easier to control than static electricity. That is why it can be used to power many objects in your home.

REAL WORLD SCIENCE CHALLENGE

Blow up a balloon and tie a string to the end. Tape the other end of the string to the top of a door frame so the balloon is hanging down with lots of room around it. Blow up a second balloon and hold it in your hand. Rub both balloons with a wool hat. Now move the balloon in your hand toward the hanging balloon. The hanging balloon will move away in the opposite direction! Why did the balloons push away from each other?

(Turn to page 29 for the answer)

Electrons flow more easily through some substances than others. These substances are called **conductors**. Water is a good conductor. Many metals, such as copper and silver, are also good conductors. If you

The plastic coating around these wires prevents shocks.

could see inside a lamp cord, you would see metal wires. The electrical wires in your house are all made of metal. The metal wires are all covered with a plastic coating. That is because plastic is an **insulator**. An insulator is a substance that does not let electricity flow as easily. Plastic, glass, and rubber are good insulators. Insulators protect you from getting shocked. An electric shock is caused when the electric current goes through your body.

Electrons can jump from one object to another. They can also flow in a more orderly manner through wires. All around you, electrons are on the move.

CHAPTER THREE

CURRENT EVENTS! THE NEWS ON ELECTRIC CURRENT

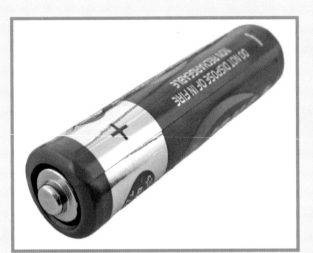

One end of a battery is positive. The other end is negative.

You can push a button to turn on the television. You can flick a **switch** and turn on a flashlight. How do they work? They need a source of power. They need a path for the electricity to travel. They also need a switch to turn the power on and off.

The source of power can be an outlet in the wall. It can also be a battery. A battery is filled with chemicals. These chemicals react to each other to create electricity. Look closely at a battery. One end is labeled positive, and one end is negative.

To create an electric current, you need to connect a wire between the

positive and negative ends. Electric current will flow through the wire. This

electric current is actually flowing electrons. The path the current travels

from the battery, through the wire, and back again is called a **circuit.**

REAL WORLD SCIENCE CHALLENGE

Take apart a flashlight and look at its parts. You'll probably see:

- Two or more batteries.
- A metal strip that starts at the bottom and runs up the inside of the flashlight.
- A switch.
- A bulb in a metal base.

Notice how the bottom battery touches the metal strip at the bottom. Notice that the metal strip leads to the switch. Notice that you can see the switch's metal piece move up and down as you flick it on and off. Notice that when you screw the top back on, the bulb base presses on the top of the second battery. How do all of these parts work together to make the flashlight work?

(Turn to page 29 for the answer)

Since you can't see inside the wire, how do you know electrons are

flowing? One way to show this is by adding a lightbulb to the circuit.

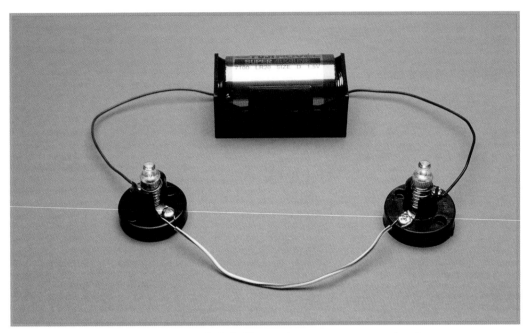

Wires connect two lightbulbs to a battery to create a circuit.

A lightbulb is made to give off light when electric current passes through

it. The wire starts at the battery and connects to the bulb. Then another

wire goes from the bulb back to the battery. The bulb will light. That is

because the bulb is along the path of flowing electrons.

If you want to turn the current on and off, you need to add a

switch to the circuit. A switch will break the circuit. This interrupts the flow of electrons. If the switch is open (or "off"), it creates a gap in the path. So the bulb will not light. If the switch is closed (or "on"), the circuit is completed. The current can then circle through the path.

In your house, the circuits are hidden behind the walls. You might have a circuit breaker in the basement or at the side of the house. This is where power enters your house. Wires lead from the circuit breaker to the wall outlets. The cord plugged into the outlet leads to a bulb in a lamp. You complete the circuit when you switch the lamp on.

Learning & Innovation Skills

You can create your own circuit experiments at home. Check the Internet or visit a local library to find easy-to-follow experiments. Remember, electricity can be dangerous. You need to get your supplies from a hobby shop. Always use plastic-coated wire and a low-voltage battery. Using the proper equipment and following directions closely will keep you safe.

When you flip a light switch, you complete a circuit, and the lights come on.

Each time you flick a switch, you complete a circuit. You just need a

power source and a complete path for the electricity to flow.

CHAPTER FOUR

COME ON OVER!
HOW MAGNETS WORK

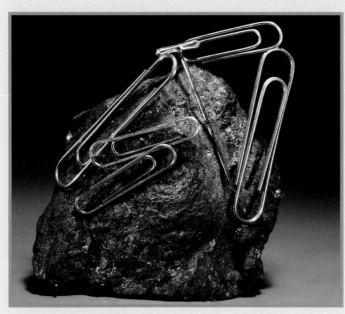

Lodestone (pictured) is a natural magnet.

Is your refrigerator covered with magnets? They seem to hold up papers like magic. Try to stick the magnet on a wooden cabinet or tile floor. It won't work. It only sticks to the metal refrigerator door.

A magnet is an object that attracts other objects. Not all magnets look like the kind on your fridge. Some magnets can be found in nature. Lodestone is a natural magnet. It is a black stone that pulls iron objects to it. Other magnets are made by people. These are made of iron, steel, or other metals mixed with iron. They come in many shapes and sizes. Some are shaped like horseshoes. Others are shaped like bars or discs.

All magnets, no matter what shape or size, work in the same way. They all have a **magnetic field**. The magnetic field is the area around a magnet that draws other objects close. Let's look at the tiny world of atoms again. Each atom has its own magnetic field. An object becomes a magnet when all of the magnetic fields of its atoms point in the same direction. They all "pull" the same way.

REAL WORLD SCIENCE CHALLENGE

You can create your own magnet. All you need is a bar magnet and a nail. Stroke the nail with one of the poles of the bar magnet. Be sure to always stroke it in the same direction, not back and forth, about 30 times. Now try to pick up a paper clip with the nail. The nail has become a magnet! How did you make a magnet out of a nail?

(Turn to page 29 for the answer)

A magnet picks up iron filings.

Think of wind. You can't actually see it. But you know it is there because of the way a flag flaps or a leaf moves. That is like the magnetic field around a magnet.

You can't see it. But you know it is there because of how objects act when near it. Place a bar magnet under a piece of white paper. Shake iron filings on the paper. Gently tap it. The iron filings will settle around the magnet where the magnet's pull is strongest. The pull is strongest at the ends of a bar magnet. These areas of strongest pull are a magnet's **poles**. All magnets have a north and south pole.

What else has a north and south pole? Earth does. Earth is like a giant magnet. You can see Earth's magnetic field at work when you use a compass. A compass helps you know your direction when you are hiking or on a trip. If you hold out a compass, the magnetic needle in the compass will spin and point north. The strong magnet of Earth is affecting the tiny magnet in your compass.

REAL WORLD SCIENCE CHALLENGE

You can make a ghost seem to float in the air using a magnet. Draw a small ghost on a piece of white paper and cut it out. Tape a metal paper clip on the back. Tie a piece of thread to the paper clip. Tape down the other end of the thread to a table top. Attract the paper clip to a magnet and raise it above the table top so the string is straight. Now slowly pull the magnet away from the paper clip just a little bit. The ghost will still float. Why does it float even though the magnet is not touching the paper clip?

(Turn to page 29 for the answer)

The like poles of two bar magnets repel each other.

With electricity, like charges push away from each other. Unlike charges pull closer to each other. It is the same way with a magnet's poles. Two poles that are the same (north/north or south/south) will push away from each other. But a north and a south pole will pull closer. Try this with two bar magnets. Put one magnet's north pole near the other magnet's south pole. The two magnets will click together. But now try joining both of their north poles, or both of their south poles. They will push away.

In a MAGLEV train, magnets on the track and magnets in the train push away from each other.

This is how a magnetic levitation (MAGLEV) train works. The train seems to float above the tracks. There is a magnet in the train and a magnet on the track. They push away from each other. This makes the train levitate above the ground.

Magnets are fun to experiment with. You can try to see how many paper clips you can pick up with one magnet. You can chase one magnet with another across a table top as they push away from each other. Even small magnets contain powerful force!

CHAPTER FIVE

SUPERSTRONG! POWERFUL ELECTROMAGNETS

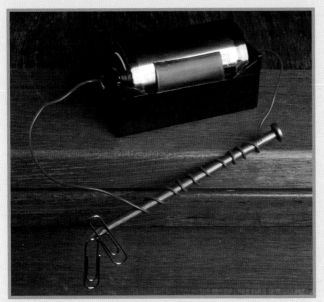

Electricity flows through a wire wrapped around a nail in this simple electromagnet.

Magnetism and electricity are not the same forces. But they are closely related. Electricity flowing through wire creates a magnetic field.

You can see this for yourself. Move a compass near a wire through which electric current is flowing. The compass needle will spin. The wire becomes a magnet. This is called an **electromagnet**.

You can make an electromagnet stronger if you coil it. You can make it even stronger if you coil it around something iron, such as a nail. This iron

The electricity you use in your home is created miles away in a power plant. A power plant uses an electromagnetic generator to create electricity. The magnet or coiled wire gets power to spin from water, wind, or steam.

The electricity then goes through power lines. The power lines lead to substations. The electricity then travels on smaller lines along poles or underground. These lines run through a transformer and finally to your house.

The wire that leads to your home goes through a meter to measure how much electricity you use. Then it goes to a circuit breaker or fuse box. Smaller wires then lead to switches and outlets in every room of your house.

center also becomes a magnet. If you put this nail near paper clips, it will pick them up. The magnet will become even stronger if you use a stronger power source to create more current.

An electromagnet works only when electricity is flowing. It stops working when you switch the power off. This makes electromagnets very useful. They can be used to run motors. A simple motor is made up of two magnets with a spinning coil of wire between them. Current passes through the wire. The coil becomes a magnet. It is pushed and pulled by the magnets around it, making it spin. This spinning motion can be used to move parts of a machine, such as a tool or a toy.

Hoover Dam generators use the power of flowing water to spin electromagnets that produce electricity.

Electricity can be used to create magnets. Magnets can also be used to create electricity. A spinning magnet near a wire can create electrical current in the wire. A spinning coil of wire surrounded by magnets can also create electrical current. A **generator** is a machine that works with this type of electromagnet. Generators are used in power plants to create the electric current we use in our homes and cities.

Think of all the items in your home that use electricity. Clocks, lights, and televisions use electricity. So does your refrigerator, stove, and dishwasher. Your hot water may be heated by electricity. Your house might be heated with electricity, too.

Sometimes the power goes out. There is no electricity getting to your home. It is good to be prepared for life without electrical power. Your family could use flashlights or candles for light. An adult could light a fire in the fireplace for heat. Canned foods and bottled water are good to have on hand for an emergency like a power outage.

It is easy to think of many uses for electricity in your home. Anything with a plug or a battery uses electricity. Electromagnets are common in many household items, too. Doorbells, refrigerators, stereos, fans, drills, toys, telephones, and even cars use electromagnets. They are also used in recycling plants to separate different kinds of metal. They are used in hospitals, too. MRI machines use magnets to create pictures of the inside of your body.

The forces of electricity and magnets are everywhere you look. Life would not be as bright, or as attractive, without electricity and magnetism!

REAL WORLD SCIENCE CHALLENGE ANSWERS

Chapter One
Page 7

The paper sticks to the television screen because of static electricity. When atoms have more electrons than protons, they become negatively charged. This is what happens on the television screen. The television screen has an excess of electrons, so it has a negative charge. This creates static electricity that holds the paper on the screen.

Chapter Two
Page 10

The water is attracted to the wand because the positive charges in the water pull closer to the negative charges in the plastic knife. When you rubbed the knife with the wool, it gained more electrons. So it has a negative charge.

Page 12

The balloons pushed away from each other because they both had the same charge. Rubbing the balloons transferred electrons from the hat to the balloons. Both balloons had extra electrons. So they both had negative charges.

Chapter Three
Page 15

A flashlight contains a complete circuit. Power flows from the bottom battery up the metal strip. When the switch is on, power flows to the metal of the bulb base. It lights the bulb and returns to the top battery. Power flows from one battery to another. When the switch is off, there is a gap in the path. No current can flow to the bulb.

Chapter Four
Page 20

The magnetic fields of the atoms in any object usually point in all different directions. By stroking the magnet on the nail, you made the magnetic fields of all the nail's atoms point in the same direction. They all "pull" the same way. That's what makes a substance magnetic.

Page 22

The paper clip on the back of the ghost is not touching the magnet. But it is still within the magnet's magnetic field. If you pull the magnet too far away, the ghost will drop down to the table.

GLOSSARY

charge (CHAHRJ) a certain amount of electricity

circuit (SIR-kut) the path a current travels from the power source, through a wire, and back again

conductors (kon-DUK-terz) substances that let electricity flow through them easily

electric current (i-LEK-trik KUR-ent) a path of flowing electrons

electromagnet (i-LEK-tro-MAG-net) a magnet created by the flow of electric current through wire

electrons (i-LEK-tronz) negatively charged particles that circle around the center of an atom

generator (JEN-er-ay-ter) a device that creates electric current by the movement of magnets and wires

insulator (IN-sul-ay-ter) a substance that does not let electricity flow through easily

magnetic field (mag-NET-ik FEELD) the area around a magnet that attracts or pushes away other objects

poles (POHLZ) the two parts of a magnet that have the strongest pull; one is the north pole, and one is the south pole

protons (PROH-TAHNZ) positively charged particles in the center of an atom

static electricity (STA-tik i-lek-TRIS-i-tee) the movement of electrons from one object to another that causes the objects to pull closer or push away from each other

switch (SWICH) a device that creates or closes a gap in an electric current

For More Information

Books

Bailey, Jacqui. *Charged Up: The Story of Electricity*. Minneapolis: Picture Window Books, 2006.

Ballard, Carol. *Exploring Electricity*. New York: PowerKids Press, 2008.

DiSpezio, Michael. *Awesome Experiments in Electricity and Magnetism*. New York: Sterling Publishing, 2006.

Parker, Steve. *Tabletop Scientist: The Science of Electricity and Magnetism*. Chicago: Heinemann, 2005.

Web Sites

The Blobz Guide to Electric Circuits
www.andythelwell.com/blobz/
Information, games, and quizzes on how circuits work

The Franklin Institute: Electrified Ben
http://sln.fi.edu/franklin/scientst/electric.html
Ben Franklin's famous electricity experiments with lightning and what he learned from them

Magnet Man: Cool Experiments with Magnets
www.coolmagnetman.com/magindex.htm
Everything you ever wanted to know about magnets, and cool magnet experiments to try what you've learned

The Shocking Truth About Electricity
http://library.thinkquest.org/6064/main.html
How electricity works, the history of its discovery, and experiments to try

INDEX

ABOUT THE AUTHOR

Dana Meachen Rau has written more than 200 books for children in preschool to middle school. Her books span subjects of science, history, geography, biography, hobbies, crafts, and reading. Every time Mrs. Rau goes on vacation, she buys a magnet to remember her trip. She keeps her magnet collection on her refrigerator in Burlington, Connecticut, where she lives with her family.